D1456798

KAYAK
SICKNESS

T. ANNIS

YSTD

DEBORAH EIBEL

KAYAK
SICKNESS

Selected Poems

1958-1971

The Sono Nis Press

BOX 94 / PORT CLEMENTS / QUEEN CHARLOTTE ISLANDS, B.C.

1972

Copyright © 1972
Deborah Eibel

All Rights Reserved

PS
8709
.I25
K3
1972

Printed in Canada by
Morriss Printing Company Ltd.
Victoria, British Columbia

For my parents and my brother

ACKNOWLEDGMENTS

Some of the poems in this volume have previously appeared in the following anthologies and magazines:

Commonwealth Poems of Today (John Murray Publisher Ltd.) 1967.
40 Women Poets of Canada (Ingluvin Press) 1971.
The McGill Poetry Chapbook (Ryerson Press) 1959.
New Poems of the Seventies (Oberon Press) 1970.
New Voices of the Commonwealth (Evans Brothers Ltd.) 1968.
PSA Diamond Anniversary Anthology (A. S. Barnes & Co.) 1971.
Soundings (House of Anansi Press) 1970.
Storm Warning (McClelland and Stewart) 1971.

Approach, The Dalhousie Review, The Greensboro Review, The Green World, The Literary Review, The Lyric, The Malahat Review, The Red Clay Reader II, The Southwest Review, The Tamarack Review.

CONTENTS

KAYAK
SICKNESS

A Dying Clown

Now he is in pain.
He is riding a midnight horse.
He is waiting for boats and for books.

Children follow with candles.
They try to bring him home.
He refuses the invitation.

He will not risk a last supper.
He has nothing more to teach.
He cannot remember the names of other clowns.

Now he is in pain.
Hosts are mysterious people.
They cannot see in the dark.

The Milliner

So little philosophy involved in her art,
But much music, much prophecy.

She is a flawless worker,
Has the spark.

Two beasts from a surrealist world
Serve as her mannequins.

The cat has the surrealist smile,
The monkey has the surrealist swagger.

The milliner has the surrealist mind
Which imposes surrealism on "tabula rasa" beasts.

Beasts with potentialities, beasts of promise,
She trains.   They make hats convincing.

Hölderlin Mad

A guest of honor
In search of a host,
In search of other guests,
He waited in the park,
Until he was called on
To close the circle.

Kaspar Hauser in Nuremberg

I

In Nuremberg
A host in search of a guest
Gave him a small room
And his first bed.

In Nuremberg
He learned to sleep, to dream, to stay awake.

Awake, he drew road-maps,
For red horses,
For royal horses.

His host read the maps
And placed wooden horses
Around the bed
Of a prince.

II

In Nuremberg
Tutors helped him.
He did his best,
So that, in time,
He was visited daily
By noisy people,
Who asked for
His drawings,
His writings,
Anything
With the signature
Of Kaspar Hauser.

III

His noisy visitors
Were uninvited —
He wanted guests.

The house in which he stayed
Was not his own —
He could not be a host.

He wanted guests,
He wanted wedding-guests.

He would not need a house
For wedding-guests.
He planned an outdoor wedding —
Under apple-trees.

A wife would come to him,
If he could learn to dance.

The Kabbalist

Because his madness had outgrown the world,
He asked the moon to magnetize his hand.
He died a fledgling, as a mystic should.
His transit leveled trees, made shadows stand.

The night he tunneled winter-to-the-moon,
A distance saints and outlaws undertake,
Disciples wept.   The scrutinist was gone:
A book would henceforth be an undragged lake.

No.   Every night he came as passerby.
His mind an anchor, he transformed their minds
Into inverted boats.   Moon-magnetized,
He mastered men and trees and birds and winds.

Kayak Sickness

The hours are curvatures, the days are rings
Concentric with the hunter of the seal;
Within the bounds of circles, he aligns
Himself with mysteries that facts conceal.

A storm is promising on August seas:
The kayak overturns; the hunter drifts
Within it, under time, locating seals;
The boat turns upright, and he claims these gifts.

Sea rage is blessed friction in the north:
It keeps a man awake to his harpoon,
Awake to nothing else.   He does not see
That sun and kayak intersect at noon.

But this is all he sees in time of calm:
On sleeping waters light obscures a map
Of mysteries so readable in storms,
And kayak embarkation is a trap.

Hypnosis is the work of light and time:
The hunter ebbs away into a cell
Within himself, away from magic seals,
Until a wind can break the hateful spell.

Of Spinsters

Their soul dies early, then it lies in state;
And flesh lives on, insensitive to loss —
When young these women dream, hear specious gloss
Of prophet birds, and so live desolate.

Especially on winter days they greet
These dark itinerants, whose wicked flight
Lures women to calamitous retreat,
Within a self as hard as anthracite.

These women have a need for amulets,
For mental talismans: in fossil bliss,
They put by unfelt joys and stock regrets,
To draw on when they wish to reminisce.

When soul long dead receives dead flesh and blood,
The anthracitic women turn to wood.

The Wind as Book

Colvin Kell, the illiterate charwoman,
Assured us that she would be
The happiest of corpses.

(We have reason to believe
Things turned out as she predicted.)

She always used the wind as book: —
This "vade-mecum" for the dying
Would, she knew,
Tell her beforehand
Of the way in which corpses are cradled.

The wind as book, she knew,
Could vouch for the experiences of corpses.

Her first concerns as corpse, she said,
Would be to find a vacant couch,
And to get accustomed
To the unfamiliar burden
Of weightless dreams.

Colvin Kell,
Who spoke in the dictum
Of those initiated by the wind,
Was convinced that the dying
Must abandon all religious pretensions: —
Corpses, she said,
Never get to touch sandals and ladders,
(The favorite symbols of those
Who imagine, in life,
That they are experiencing
A vicarious sainthood).

Colvin Kell undoubtedly became
The happiest of corpses,
Because there was a Quixotic element
In her thoughts: —
Unlike other women,
She did not worry about decorum,
About what her status as a corpse would be.

Because hers was such a miraculous simplicity,
A new season,
An auxiliary spring,
Came when she left.

The Man Who Married Colvin Kell

After a spinsterhood of many years,
Colvin Kell, the illiterate charwoman
Who spoke in the dictum
Of those initiated by the wind,
Who never worried about decorum,
Accepted the offer of an unlikely man,
One who had been rejected by other charwomen,
Because he was shiftless.
But Colvin Kell, being a grammarian among charwomen,
Could read his mind.
Because she used the wind as "vade-mecum", as gloss,
He was never too inscrutable for her.
She accepted him, because he was a whole man:
He loved caterpillar and moth and butterfly,
Wood and fire and ash.
Late marriage was meaningful
In ways that earlier marriage could not have been.
The pastimes that mattered now
Could not have mattered before.
Nothing could have mattered before.
They loved to walk in stony places:
They verified themselves by kicking stones.
They honored each other.
She kept the floors and walls and woodwork
Immaculate for him.
Delighted with her art,
He scratched "Colvin fecit"
On whatever she touched.
(These are the only words she ever learned to read.)
He paid further tribute
By playing his flute.
When she asked him
Why he repeated the melody hour after hour

Without embellishing it,
He said that for this theme
There could be no variations.
But one day, years later,
When he thought her back was turned,
He changed.
She understood what was happening.
She had known from the first
That a change must come about, sooner or later,
That he would one day lean away, break away.
(After all, had he not married beneath his station?)
That day, he did not ask her to go walking with him,
But she left the kitchen anyway and followed at a distance.
There were stones on the road;
He walked around them instead of kicking them.
He embellished the flute melody,
For which, he had said before,
There could be no variations.
It was dark, it was raining, he was old.
He agreed to come home.
He went to sleep.
Colvin Kell knew that he was searching
For a carnival place, for hilarity.
They would not meet again, anywhere.
(She did not mean that he was necessarily lost,
For he had not been a worthless man.
But there would always be distance between them.)

Just before he left,
All seasons converged on his tongue.
After his departure, they realigned themselves.

Early Sorrow

The traveler always writes first —

Whenever the musical cousin is away,
He writes long letters,
Which his noisy cousins never answer.
But he thinks he is their traveler —
They want him to travel for them,
They expect him to be different
When he comes back.
He is the only cousin who pretends.

Last night the noisy cousins met him
At Grand Central Station.
Today they are all playing together
On a lawn at Sheepshead Bay.
The noisy cousins always say:
"You are very tired".
They give him a headstart in the race.

Now it is raining,
So they cannot finish.
But they never finish,
When the musical cousin is there.
Some one always says:
"Let's play school".
The musical cousin is always the teacher.

He is the only one who pretends.
He tells them everything
They could possibly want to hear.
In a way, he is their traveler.
Every one looks forward to seeing him again.

Syllogism

My darling,
The journal I kept when young,
That kept me from coming of age,
That had meaning for none but prophet birds,
Has been in the ocean for years.

Let me keep another;
It will be different from the first.
I shall make a compendium of syllogisms.

Here is the first one:
All wives of clowns dance beautifully for their husbands;
I am the wife of a clown;
Therefore I dance beautifully for my husband.

Of Children Who Keep Journals

In Brooklyn there are children who keep journals.
On sand, on boardwalk, and on fire-escape
They work, in any season.   Day and night
They chronicle processions, structure myths.

We are of value to the sidestreet children
Who make a casebook on our handball games,
Our costume parties, and our subway rides,
Who structure all the myths that we involve.

They do not speak with us they write about,
They do not play with other sidestreet children.
And were it not for pages that get lost,
We would not even know that they keep journals.

In Brooklyn there are children who keep journals,
On sand, on boardwalk, and on fire-escape.

The Visit

On fire-escape, on boardwalk, and on sand,
I kept a journal, even during winter.
A makeshift child, how should I understand
That all my structured myths would one day splinter?

Last night I brought my journal to your attic.
"My prophet bird, your journal is your cage,"
You said.   "It makes you sorcerous, fanatic.
No prophet bird has ever come of age.

"But you, my love, will come of age, tonight.
Come down to Brighton Beach, and let us quarrel,
Then kiss and play.   And nothing will you write,
But throw your book away, lock, stock, and barrel,

"And live, determined as a meteor.
Your myths are in the sea now, far from shore."

Roots

"New tenants have arrived" —
Before and after class
The sidestreet children play
Outside the boardinghouse.

The mothers disapprove:
Their bedtime serenades
Concern the boulevards
In better neighborhoods.

The children do not heed
The serenade advice:
That strangers come to them
Is reason not to leave.

But sometimes, when in doubt,
They talk to famous men,
To actors, generals —
New tenants in the slums —

Who tell of boulevards
They left behind for good,
The day they found a street
Too narrow for parades.

No traveler should
Continue indefinitely
On the same road.

I recall that,
As a child,
I craved a symmetry
In my wanderings.

I chose a straight road,
With poplars to my right
And poplars to my left,
A straight road
With ancient purple stones
To my right and to my left.

Then came the winter
Of young womanhood.
Heavy snow covered
My straight road.
It covered my poplars
And my purple stones.
The symmetry of childhood
Was concealed.

I tried at first
To shovel all the snow away;
It blinded me,
I knew this snow would always stay.

I found a better road,
A crooked road this time.

And yet I think that other road was kind,
The road that was in league with blinding snow.
It taught me that a traveler
Can outgrow a road.

Winterreise

Unfurnished rooms
Need illnesses.

From time to time
We put our books away,
We close our eyes,
We contract illnesses.

We name our illnesses,
We pass them on to guests,
To disciples.

They know us by our illnesses,
By our way of surviving
In unfurnished rooms.

Death of a Goldfish

Adventure was reduced within the bowl:
A golden fish was dying.   There could be
No good recovery for him whose soul
Played aimlessly below his private sea.

He must have heard the music of a glass
Guitar, a dirge without an echo, tossed
Against him when his body turned to brass,
And meanings of his life-in-gold were lost.

The death experience of fish, alone
In private seas, is sad.   They fall on sands
Not made for dreams, and there they turn to stone,
And lie unconscious of Redeeming Hands.

Adventure is no longer in that cove
Where gentle-rhythmed goldfish loved to move.

A Clown in History

Be patient.   He is not a drunken exile,
A runaway.   The circus is his classroom.
A good historian, he plans his lessons.
Through him we witness birth and death of epochs.

This act is not for those who love commotion.
The silent clown does little more than signal
"Good-morning" and "good-night".   He enters sleeping.
The playful clowns depart.   All music stops.

The clown has been asleep, he enters sleeping.
He never oversleeps.   Now it is morning:
He wakes us up, because we too were sleeping.
We know that something is about to happen —

Exactly what, we are not meant to know.
What matters is that we are drawn together.
The clown can make us feel that we are part
Of some new movement, part of history.

The clown is overjoyed at our response —
We understand his act.   But suddenly
He turns away from us and falls asleep.
An era having passed, he exits sleeping.

We sleep, until the clown reenters sleeping
And wakes us up.   He has good news . . . and so on.
Tonight he made us part of many movements,
And he will teach like this until his doomsday.

The Simple Last Hours of an Obscure Saint

A simple hour, and reptile clouds
Invaded attics of the sky;
A forest saint compared two paths
And chose a silent place to die.

A hermit and a fallen tree:
He hailed it Dreaming Skeleton —
It seemed his shadow.   Both were black
Against white birch, the forest nun.

A silent place, his place to die:
Along the ground each leaf he met
Lay vicar of a season's god —
Some leaf which had not fallen yet.

A sparrow died; the saint gave up
A last, a simple hour, to sit
And mourn this tiny death.   He knew
His own death soon would echo it.

A simple hour to end his walk:
The chill of infant night enthralled
Him.   Attics of the sky came down
And reptile clouds about him crawled.

The hermit, in his dying, knew
The forest sky should never rest
If stars returned each night, to play
Upon that day-rubbed palimpsest.

A simple hour: the dying saint
Recalled the night he left the sea
To build a forest hut, and have
The moon appraise his carpentry.

Tonight the moon as forester
Came down to greet the hermit, put
Herself into a barque of clouds
And led the saint into his hut.

The simplest hour, his hour to die:
The hermit stretched his arm — an oar
Of withered flesh — and with his tools
He nailed a flower to the floor.

He nailed a flower, nailed a prayer —
A gentle rite.   Old trees began
To lean upon his hut — they knew
Man followed tree, tree followed man.

Hagar to Ishmael

Come out of the shrubs now,
My Ishmael,
Come out of the shrubs.
The road to death
Becomes again
The road to Egypt.

When we ran out of water and bread,
My Ishmael,
Out of water and bread,
I sensed suddenly
That fear of music
Had overtaken the wilderness of Beersheba —
Fear that turned to hate:
There was no echo
When I sang
A Canaanite lullaby.
The wilderness had rejected
My song, me, us.

When I sensed this,
My Ishmael,
When I sensed this,
I became a coward,
And you, therefore,
Became an orphan:
I left you in the shrubs
And would not watch you die.
But God made the wilderness
Love music again,
And He made me brave enough
To take you out of the shrubs.

So now that we are together again,
My Ishmael,
Together again,
Let us consider your future.
God warned me once in Shur,
That my son would be recalcitrant.

But if it is up to me,
My Ishmael,
Up to me,
You will have no reason
To be recalcitrant.

I shall not force you,
My Ishmael,
Not force you,
To assume unnecessary responsibilities.
We shall leave such things
To Isaac, your illustrious half-brother.
Your genius is for archery:
I know this, Ishmael.
You have always studied
The movements of beasts
And the contours of the wilderness:
You have the makings
Of a great archer.

One thing more,
My Ishmael,
Just one thing more: —
We shall walk slowly to Egypt,
More slowly than you may consider necessary.
There is a reason for walking slowly: —

Remember that God is the vessel,
Time the thing contained.
Now time often flees its vessel,
And mockingly challenges it
To a race.
In such a race as this
God deliberately lags behind.
You and I must wait for God,
My Ishmael,
Must wait for God.

A New Era

On the way home from school this afternoon,
The children explore old hiding-places,
Where they will never play again.

Tomorrow morning the face of the city will change suddenly,
And traffic will be rerouted
To make way for new heroes.
The children will have to look for new hiding-places.

On the way home from school this afternoon,
The children sing in unison, in tune:
This is choral music.
The children are together,
Because an era is drawing to a close.

In no house are there dinner guests this evening.
For some time now, members of the immediate family
Have had nothing to say,
Not even to one another.

Heroes of the passing era used to be invited.
Now the back door is locked,
Because heroes who want to stay behind
Have a way of reentering a house
By the back door.

Tomorrow morning heroes of a new era
Will ring the front doorbell.
The children, looking forward to a new day,
Prepare the kites they have not played with lately.
They clear the long-neglected front doorstep
Of winter overshoes.

Work and Play

This is a broken home.
A child is playing.
When his father is away,
He rearranges his bedroom furniture —
He receives wicked visitors.

These are his father's wicked relatives.
They ask about the handmade things —
Bookmarks, maps, mobiles.
They ask him
Why he works so hard,
Why he works
While others play.

This is a broken home.
He has become a good listener —
His wicked relatives keep reminding him
That his father used to play
While others worked.

Chairs

Left out of schoolyard games,
A child consoles himself:
"Impatient children know
They can depend on me.

"They know I wish them well —
But they are busy now
And cannot be my guests.
One day they will have time.

"I have begun to furnish
A room.   My friends will come,
And some will sit in arm-chairs,
And some in rocking-chairs."

"Must everything of value have a center?"
Asked gifted children exiled in the West —
Each one an echo and a palimpsest.

They dreamed of strongholds they would never enter,
Of Tel-Aviv, a town without a center —
Unless that center were a central park.

They verified their daydreams in the dark —
They dreamed of strongholds they would never enter.

My father prophesied for other children;
For love of strangers he neglected me —
(As if a prophet should neglect his own
And go away to teach in distant households!)

My father prophesied in many cities,
And younger citizens who would escape
He led into his native wilderness.
These other children were his only heirs.

Perhaps I failed my father.   City-born,
I never went into his wilderness,
I never went away to distant cities.
My father had to live for other children.

Perhaps my father might have learned from me.
A gifted child, I had a following —
The citizens, whose lives I cared about.
I was the neighborhood chronologer.

My father hated cities.   He disowned me,
Not caring how I grew in school and schoolyard.
But now, an old man in a central park,
I wish that I had been his only heir.

My Father, Playing Father

My father, playing father, held my hand —
A visitor, about to leave again
To teach in distant households of our land.
He left, and took a shortcut through the lane.

My father, playing father, made me cry —
He never let a secret leave his throat;
For strangers only did he prophesy;
He came home only when the overcoat

In which he pilgrimed had to be repaired,
The emblem of desertion.   And my mother,
Despite the laughter of the neighbors, spared
No pains for him; she would not love another.

My father, playing father, played the clown —
He prophesied for children not his own.

Homecoming

Though none has ever bothered to molest
The unmet lady getting off the train,
She still has guilty dreams within her breast,
For nutriment.   But she is porcelain,
For want of love.   Now, on this harvest night,
Her country birthplace lies in savage ease.
On porches, in a wilderness of spite,
Her cousins revel in their strategies.
Their words incriminate the innocent —
And so she is a spinster.   Yet, in fall,
She comes with no particular intent,
To visit kin — a harmless ritual.
And, palpable, she speaks.   But kin are deaf
To one who comes unbidden as a leaf.

Doomsday Dancing

World history
Is the doomsday passion
Of the mad.
Today, in Akko,
Having survived the last khamsin,
All madmen,
The first and the last,
Natives and newcomers,
Are contemporaries.
They are recording world history
As a dance.

World history
Is a doomsday passion.
Today, in Akko,
Madmen are dancing
Among the royal snails,
The purple snails —
They are looking for sleepwalkers,
For exiled teachers,
Who no longer know them.

The sermons
Madmen ran away from
Are still beautiful.

It is doomsday in Akko.
Having survived the last khamsin,
Madmen are free
To discover,
To choose.

Beowulf Remembered

In parishes along the northern bays,
Old men claim shells are maddened; regiments
Of shells lie breathless on the beach, and talk
At random of the wilderness of seas.

Their huge lips give a terror to the ear
Of timid noon.   Yet speak they must; those shells
That make a silent kingdom of the sand
Are punished by the wind and thrown away.

But most endure; and each of these recites
Its private version of the history
Of champions who lived along the bays,
Of Beowulf, who played with maddened shells.

Scene of King Harold's Death Revisited

We quarried dead laws out of dusk
And played beside their maker; slain,
He saw, in forests pilgrimless,
Hardrada cowering in the rain.

No Normans found he wheeling there,
No war-cry shook that ancient yard,
Yet heard he wails of harpless souls —
The sparrow was a Saxon bard.

First, winter dropped on panes of leaf,
— We heard the mouths of woodstreams close:
The Witenagemot lay dumb
With Harold, in the granite snows.

When Knight Rinaldo turned away from war,
Such was the nature of this pilgrim's search
That roads were holy, though Cologne was far;
And, nameless in Cologne, he built a church.

He hesitated when the workmen asked
His name and history; none understood
This man who took no wage, this martyr masked;
Hence clouds were painted with Rinaldo's blood.

And splintered night put down this anecdote:
The dreams Rinaldo cellared in his heart
Were damaged when the masons tore his throat,
More jealous of his faith than of his art.

But penance had prepared him to succumb
To this, the lighted cage of martyrdom.

He did not wince, when desert eagles towered
Like braggarts in the heated sky.   His head
Was like a tarnished orb.
                              The desert flowered
Invisibly : — aware of this he said :
"I thought my agonies would make me harden
And make me shrink.   Instead the discipline
Has made a giant of me.   In this garden
I, Anthony, shall rest my giant chin
On giant palms.   But first I must surrender
My ancient earthly garments.
                              "Brethren, are
Such garments not the seals of simple splendor?"
(These clothes had also been his calendar
Of desert months and years.)
                              He shut his lids
And soon forgot about the pyramids.

We slept on this island, all afternoon.
We rarely conversed.
Giving, taking —
Soon we were taught
By a guest,
An invader,
An enemy.

Then we imprisoned
The traveler who landed,
The teacher who came,
Lest he abandon us.

Our faces changed.
Our prisoner waited
For converts to free him.

The Wife of Rabbi Israel ben Eliezer

He scrutinized the movements of a feather —
Essentially she was his weathervane —
Then hastened to negotiate the rain,
To carry out his mission in bad weather.

She let him go, because she was angelic.
That day, because he prospered in his search
For souls imprisoned, he outdanced a birch
And left it lying breathless as a relic.

For love of her, his dancing was outspoken.
Because he had a loudness of the bones,
The world undid itself.   In rain, the stones
And other prisons waited to be broken.

A Passion for Diving

My imagination
Is underwater,
In a music room.

There are many
Underwater music rooms
In the Atlantic Ocean.

My family and friends
Have learned to welcome me
To *terra incognita*.
I have become a guest —
They want me to survive.

I have been learning so much —
How to drown,
How to be disappointed.

I must keep losing myself
In my underwater music room.
Phantom pain
Makes me talk to strangers,
To hosts,
On *terra incognita*.

St. Jerome the Translator

During my desert years
I learned another language —
I needed passwords,
And I found them
In the dark.

Now I live in Bethlehem.
I have brought
All my books of knowledge
To this small room —
At times it has four corners,
At times it has a hundred.

I am still a vegetarian,
I fast until sunset.
I will try to stay here
For a long time,
Forty years, if necessary,
In order to map maps —
This is safe work
For a magus
Whose lyric impulse
Is so strong.
I do not always trust
My homing ability.

Hotel St. George, Brooklyn Heights

The subway stops downstairs,
Below the lobby.
It is the first station in Brooklyn
For trains from Manhattan.

Upstairs, in the lobby,
Are famous traveling actors
Who finally came home, with good stories,
And found the doors locked.
Lost ambassadors, condemned grandfathers
Tell each other hundreds of stories
They wanted to tell at home.

They play a hospitality game.
They listen to each other,
They memorize what they hear.
Each is a homeless host,
A homeless guest.

Eve and Her Husband Shortly After the Fall

Another home,
  This far-from-Eden yard,
God found for them.
  There nothing could retard

Their dancing hearts.
  And concave Eve came close
To him and sang
  Of children — ariose,

That song to him
  And to his acorn-rib.
He understood,
  He made a leafy crib.

When Eve said, "Come",
  He roused himself, said, "Yes".
His mind was new,
  His mind was Edenless.

His mind was now
  An archipelago:
He scouted it
  And watched new islands grow.

This convex man
  Came to her: "I salute
Thee, rib and wife.
  Now let us greet the fruit

Of exile, greet
  The fruit of our new pain."
The convex man
  Bent down and gave her Cain.

Freethinkers

Holy men
Have been known to endorse
The dancing of freethinkers.

There are freethinkers
Among the bereaved grandfathers
Of Haifa.
After the war
They gave up listening to good music —
The rhythms of grief
Are somewhere on noisy streets.
The rhythms of grief
Are the essential liturgy.

It is midnight in Haifa:
The freethinkers
Among the bereaved grandfathers
Are dancing, hand in hand,
Down a noisy street,
To the rhythms of grief.
They always stay out late.
They have become a new underworld.

No Forerunners

Now that the city is safe,
Public speakers from the desert
Are rare.

The few who do enter the city
Cannot find a crowd
Waiting to be rescued.
And so they look for work.
Few leave.

Long ago,
They would have been forerunners.
They would have brought news,
Made promises.

Now that the city is safe,
I, a citizen,
Can choose my auditors,
One by one.
I want no desert forerunners,
No reputation.

No one ever calls me
Latecomer.

A Young Swallow Laments His Inability to Improvise

The others have denounced me now,
Because of darkness in my throat;
I have no music of my own —
I learn to sing old songs by rote.

I am a plagiary bird —
An echo and a travesty
Of other swallows.   I annul
The sounds they drop on rock or tree.

I am a source of wilderness,
Because I cannot improvise;
The tragic hardness in my voice
Is plummet torturing the skies.

Absalom Ballads

Were Prince Absalom to return,
He would move to Tel-Aviv,
Without asking his father's permission.

In no time,
He would become
A popular soldier-poet.

In a certain café without a name on the door,
He would work to the accompaniment of jazz.
He would write haunting ballads
About fathers and sons,
In slang Hebrew.

Prince Absalom's favorite café
Would become known as
"Absalom's Place".

This Courtship, This Chiasmus

Drowsily we build
A steepled mountain:
My last word
You take up as your first;
My first word
Becomes your last.
I am words and music;
You are my echo in reverse.
I am an adventure;
You are that adventure in reverse.
Such is our courtship,
Our chiasmus.

The Acrobat on his Deathbed

Last night I tabernacled in the air
With music for a ladder, and I met
A gilded host — my sons were leaping there
Like sails a stricken boat had lost.   They let
Me join them as they fled some heaving sea.
Now sail, not ship, sees the horizon first.
Thus, as I leapt, those weathers which to me,
As sea-nailed ship, seemed in their distance cursed
With black, now turned to sun, a sun in night,
So long as I remained a sail and leapt.
But since I was an ancient sail, the light
Of good horizons dimmed.   As ship I slept.
My sons did not come down.   That gilded host
Stayed in the sky as sails — the sky I lost.